I0888926

Blood Mother

Blood Mother

Su Croll

John Barton, Editor

Signature
EDITIONS

Cover art © Betty Goodwin, Untitled (from "Swimmers" series), 1982; photo © National Gallery of Canada, Ottawa
Cover design by Doowah Design.
Photo of Su Croll by jalleyne.

This book was printed on Ancient Forest Friendly paper.
Printed and bound in Canada by Marquis Book Printing Inc.

We acknowledge the support of The Canada Council for the Arts and the Manitoba Arts Council for our publishing program.

Acknowledgements
Earlier versions of some of these poems were first published or broadcast in the following: *Stroll of Poets: the 1999 Anthology; Take the Poetry Route* (a project on Edmonton transit buses and LRTs); *Room of One's Own; Event; Other Voices; CV2; Arc;* CBC's *Alberta Anthology;* and *The Antigonish Review.* Thanks to the editors and organizers. Thanks also to my friend Arlene Tyo for the conversation about French grammar that led to "translation." Thank you to Karen Haughian at Signature Editions in Winnipeg. I am especially grateful to John Barton for his insightful and exacting work as my editor. Finally, I would like to thank my husband, Wayne Murdoch: I couldn't have done it without you.

Library and Archives Canada Cataloguing in Publication

Croll, Su, 1961–
Blood mother / Su Croll.

Poems.
ISBN 978-1-897109-27-4

1. Motherhood—Poetry. I. Title.

PS8555.R596B56 2008 C811'.54 C2008-905485-7

Signature Editions
P.O. Box 206, RPO Corydon, Winnipeg, Manitoba, R3M 3S7
www.signature-editions.com

for Wayne
Lizzie and Duncan

Contents

roof of clouds net of stars

drinking the light

persistence of vision

projection

my mother in pregnancy
her body revealed
shaped in the rush of wind
moving her hair and pushing her
clothes against the body that holds me

she turns and speaks to the camera   silent
but for the ticking of 8mm film
rattling the gate of the bell
and howell projector   24 frames
per second   there are 24 small squares
rushing headlong into the light
shaping a single instant

96 frames of bright fluttering to reveal
scant fluid seconds of my mother
pulling off her 1960s silver cat-glasses
a flourish of wrist and arm and she laughs
head thrown back as wind catches
her hair   as light
pulses the white wall
holding this flickering

image as it moves
a wavering colour
projection of my pregnant
mother wringing the last light
of memory from this fragile vein
of 48-year-old film stock
where I steal a fleeting image
of myself

unborn

fruitful

desire made flesh

how desire forces itself
how the limits of our bodies can
not be reached and our lives revolve
around the coiled spiral of an ovulation calendar

how we are taken over   urgent
for the future   multiple
threads have knotted   have braided themselves
into ropes between us   through the years

strands have thickened   our flesh
connection solidifying to bone and muscle
and heart   the sudden web of the heart strung along

beating blood pathways   a tapestry of entwined flesh
forced into the lush uterine bed to weave
40 burgeoning weeks into our bodies' desire

alphabet

the image all by itself
lying across the horizon
of the line   the lip
of the next riding up
to compress the picture
this is how we house pregnancy
and how pregnancy houses us
as each word   each key
stroke   each flick and pull
of the page makes letters
and their meanings inhabit the book
of the body   each printing brands
this sudden kick
start as life   the beginning
of life gets its hooks into us
the body becomes narrative
unfolding   a steady accruing of detail
at 2 weeks it is smaller than the letter
"a" on this page and I anticipate
blood   am infused
with enriched letters growing into
a word bathed in fertility
becoming the smallest subject
for poetry   this budding fruit
of the abundance of my belly
this possibility and me
peeking through the smallest door
smallest window in the house
to the world outside this box of heat
until the alphabet is complete

annunciation

december 13 ultra sound dates me nine weeks
ballooned full of water   my secret is revealed
what the technician names *baby*
a white throbbing
sheltering under my pelvic bone   *the heart*
he raises his hand   palm up
that's the heart

december 13   feast day of st lucia

her name suggests what is lucid
what is light and what can be seen
in light   on this dark december morning
a child is suggested

no   st lucia's day reaches beyond
suggestion   ultra sound is simple
truth   an illuminated manuscript
the story of this life inscribes itself

inside my body where a second heart blooms
and I see flashing like lightning
what will be a baby   a curled near-nothing
through the magnifying gold
fish bowl of my bladder   so many clear
glasses of water inflating me into a phantom

of pregnancy as it will not be seen
till spring and there is this water lily
this fish of a child   my child
floating on a soft curve of spine
and it is the heart that is first visible
on this day suddenly sacred to sight

fruitful

we are fallen into words
flimsy female language
a dialect of oranges and asters
we say flowery because of the light
insubstantial   purple   swollen
plums of language that are read
as purple prose and to be newly
in leaf and blossom   to be fresh
picked   a budding rose
is to be light   womanly
there is no non-gendered language
though even the presence of the word
gender and its other
hidden face already weigh down
this leafy construction   I am left
wordless   unable to explain
my fertile ovulating conceiving gestating
labouring delivering lactating
body   I should stop
trying for more formidable words
more heavyweight dialogue
because the language of vegetation
of fruit and flowers   of ocean
and moon is the shape women have
taken in language   our blood clichéd
and rooting us to nature
the only way we can be
described

pressed flower

expecting a baby in two weeks
living narrowly   listening to the washing
machine spin out baby
clothes in preparation   I am making
a child to fill this flat and folded
fabric   as they hang
to dry   air opens and closes
the sleeves and neck openings
breathes over and through clothing
that has yet to touch
the baby
housed in my still
closed body
the empty house is filled
with the smell of soap and I wonder
if the sleepers and socks and soft
cotton undershirts themselves
will soon shut me off
from the world as I ready myself
for the wringer   a compression
within walls   I am thinking
of a victorian flower press though all
images are thrown
off kilter   the walls are biological
the press is the process
where I will find myself
between the suddenly close
walls of a secret room I have
never known at the centre
of my house as if
the birth will be my own
and not given
to a child I must prepare
to mother

pickles

they say to carry a jar of pickles
you can drop if you are concerned
about your water breaking at a bus stop
or in the line-up at safeway
if you are worried what is inside
with shame and abruptness will spring
a leak and flood outside   water
once a stormless ocean
in your belly   bursting free
and flowing to your ankles
that round jar of kosher dills salty
salvation pulled from inside your coat
and thrust to the sidewalk as your own
brine stains your underwear   I'm picturing
some kind of harpo-marx coat stuffed
with rubber chickens and uncoiling
slinky snakes and you are
saved as glass and vinegar and cucumbers
smash away from themselves   that delicious
splash of acid and salt coating your tongue
from the crash and you laugh
you dropped the jar while it is the drip
then bursting dam of your own kid
you are ready to drop

what I forget

I forget my first labour and all its fury
they say we forget what the body must
how fury slides spent
from slick skin but not from muscle-memory
of pain buried beneath skin and embedded in bone
to be held until the end   they say we forget
pain and the beginning of pain   we are told
not to invoke that underworld demon
all black heat and surgically sharp teeth
or it will burst the cervical maw
of the wet earth and gnash and tear
the labouring muscle we become
the whole 12 or 24 or 36 hours it takes
for labour to rumble through and consume

but that's wrong   pain is not born
inside the earth   it's all mine   my own
offspring gestating inside this closed
grenade of a womb until the barrage begins

I am taught not to call on the pain
inside   pain is old

an old-fashioned word cautions the nurse
at labour and delivery class where I learn
the fury of the body in labour as I crush
my husband in the feathered embrace
of practice pillows and learn the breathing
meant to hold my head above
the coming tide

I am taught
it is *pain with a purpose*   I am told
to visualise some serene ocean
swimming up and out of itself

I am given a focal object
a stone   a feather   a photograph of the near
invisible cleft of water and sky washed

grey-blue a photograph my clamped
shut eyes don't see as pain blossoms
purple then red a sea demon churning the air
of the labour room my body is swallowed into
back on land a man is counting every throbbing
breath saw-toothed numbers
ferrying me up the crest of every
spiked contraction as labour crashes
the shipwreck I become
and though taught not to I cover myself
with its furious tearing sails I splinter out
into several spiralling directions on the skin
surface of this and my body calls pain to itself
in a voice I cannot recognize as my own

while he counts my broken breath

and in the troughs between waves
I tread water my hands makeshift nets
forgetting what I'm fishing for

I forget everything
the pulsing red-walled labour room
the man clenching my shoulders whispering
a soft incantation of wind into my face
while I grasp at numbers
that have no meaning

at the centre of pain I forget

I forget I'm inside the body's fury

my body
my fury

I forget the child relinquishing
her amniotic inland sea and I float
free of the sutured surface
and all pain
all fury is forgotten

lungs forced open

receiving

a reservoir of the world
wide as this room where the palm
of a parent is shaping
a cup of air as it nears
the back of an infant's head
richest moment of our lives
her head   heaviest
part of the body   our hearts
now fully open
covering of soft new bone
cradled in our wondering hands

gift

as if she were a gift   as yet unopened
and I could look but not touch   not have
as if I needed to ask permission
to have her in my room alone
all night   as if I did not have a right
to her   as if she were not mine
but she was   my own child
so barely in the world   she seemed not real
not really here   a swaddled stranger   I needed
to ring for the nurse to give me my child
as if she were an unopened gift though it was me
opened and this gift   this daughter
so recently cut and plucked out of me
I thought I needed to ask to have the child
my sudden child placed in my arms
when only hours before
she had been sharing my blood
sheltered in me   the same as me
only hours before   she was me
not yet in my arms and I was not yet a mother
and as a mother   so newly a mother
I didn't know I didn't have to ask

first night

on the first night I told my daughter
I was her mother   I told
my daughter as I tried to learn to hold her
and nurse her and quiet her crying
a crying that would translate
into a knowable vocabulary of need

but that night I had not yet learned the dialect
could only hold her and watch her breathe
and sleep knowing I was already tangled up
with the rhythms of her still foreign body

I had my own sleep broken apart
every hour by her wordless
wanting of me

though she could not fathom
the geography of my face
she already had my voice
imprinted on her from five months' gestation
hearing my voice through the pulsing
screen of placenta and the walled
fortress of my body

now she was netted
by the smell
of the milk knitting us together

alive for less than a day
my mouth close to her sleeping face
I taught my infant daughter the order
of the world   I told her I was hers
I told her I was
her mother and that I would be her mother
forever   I would be her mother
after my death

choice

I arrive at choice
previously unspoken
a poem about how
I want motherhood
to be a decision
in this world cross-
stitched with meaning   I'm
threading lines   embroidering
a blunt red circle around this
word   so fingers
running over the skin
of this page will read *choice*
by touch   red letters
appliqued with the symbol
for choice   the *yes* I made
to that pearl   that soft shell
unformed self as it once
bathed in my salt water
now it is choice
lying here in my arms
how I chose to carry
myself through
the world with this other
within me and now
I embrace
what we have sown
embrace this small
new light

the weight of sleep

sleep enters her mouth
her bones are water
logged with sleep   blood
dense in her muscles   the ocean
floor of sleep a magnet drawing
her deeper   the air
expands with sleep until she eases it
back into herself on the hook
of her inhaled breath   sleep
reddens and fills each muscle
sleep snakes through her
feeding her blood
I hold her as she falls
into sleep   as she grows
heavy in my arms and her fists
open   uncurl and her breathing
deepens and everything
everything is the body
her body   my own
body altered   my centre changed
until I am helpless and circling
the planet that is this tiny
girl   I ache
radiating from the marrow
of my bones to the blood
throbbing my muscles to the sheath
of my skin   a sweet ache
binding us   my body
shaped to hers

enfleshment

half way between my body and the world
my daughter's eight day-old dreams
enacted upon her sleeping face

in sleep her face rehearses
all faces she will ever need
all possibility hovering over her

a future an imagined future animating
her unknowing face her dreams
are of the mouth she is a human

shaped animal taking animal bliss
whole-body bliss through her ravenous
mouth hunger

retreating against abundance flowing
through her lips and throat
and I am caught in her circular need

emptying into her immaculate
mouth I fall asleep and she is lifted
away I still drink in her

radiating heat breathe with her
dream of being grafted to her
when she breathed only my blood

thrummed her fingers only to my beating
heart and I feast
on the vision of my daughter's face

I don't know how to free these words
from my mouth I know the mouth
the latch of her mouth as a sacrament

a deal we make with the world
to come I will give you
this milk I will give you this

blood this bone and flesh

sucking

I need to be literal
at the beginning of every life there is nothing

but sucking   sucking is instinct
survival   taking that jet of hot milk

shot into the mouth and learning
to swallow in the world

no metaphor can encompass
outside the wet of the womb

learning to swallow
before the mouth

overfills   the world is held
in suction   there is

no metaphor
for milk   there is only this

hard language of demand
there is only the breast answering

I need
to be literal   all life

craves   I want
this line unadorned

want it to tell what is
true and essential

the final thick cream
of the emptying breast

plush

the pleasure of her body in my arms
and the pleasure that is her light
fingertip touch   I am consumed

the measured waiting for morning as it flows
into the room   coffee poured over warmed
milk   fragrant roses languid
lingering in the air   our daughter
enraptured   the leisure of waiting
for the blush of daybreak to touch her face

the flux of light on the milk-white wall
the delirious fragrance   those flowers
adding to the immeasurable content of a day

built around the lilt of light
waking and sleeping and the rapture
of our daughter's face and moving fingers
stilled with the fading of light then the pleasure
my husband and I take as we fall away together
pressed together   his out-of-focus body
his body a ghost presence   a measure of comfort

a pleasure remembered in these thin still
seconds before the plush of sleep crushes us
into its velveteen embrace and all night
I dream of the pleasure of her body in my arms

aperture

though I stare all day
I can't fix her face in my mind as she shimmers
radiant with the flickering motion of hundreds
thousands of distinct glimmering frames rewinding
to that curled-up infant of only 5 weeks ago

everyday I plan to write but can't
focus on her face and fall into autobiography
I speed into the future   moment to moment
memory snapping forward   a blinding
staccato of flashbulbs   I want to remember

everything   hold these kinetic days
still in my hands but time is quick
silver and my daughter is multiple
pictured keepsake seconds

I'm fused to her and I can't see   can't
capture a single snapshot as we race ahead
no image holds up   the slippery nature
of the present swathes us in absolute

fluidity and can't be fixed onto paper

lungs forced open

as if accuracy were an end in itself
I don't know how to live

I don't know clocks and I don't
know leaves   yellow in the wide

flat palm of prairie to foot
hills I am living in   I don't know

what part of the country from colours
practically unfamiliar   what time

of day   what season   I barely know
my husband at this altitude

in this west   how he lives
and moves through the high

and dry of this air   he walks
across a river to a downtown

job I can't imagine   I don't
know how to live   there's breathing

and eating and looking at yellow
trees before wind takes

their leaves   I don't know
how the television can

stand itself   brewing pictures
frenzied crowds forcing open

locked doors   I don't
know how the barricades

can endure   I only know
my stubborn stretched skin

barricading the body and life
forcing itself on a flesh

coloured wind of shrill
oxygen into my daughter's open

mouth the moment she was pulled
blue from my slit

open
abdomen   that slim red

scalpel line marking me
in that second before life begins

with breathing
I don't know anything

but the body   the body
of this western city   the country

of my own body   residence of my daughter
my heart

erratic

the wind is a sky-coloured memory of that day
        the anomaly of the big rock
a wedge of mountain pulled to earth eons
        before our births
when will there ever be another time when we have so much
        access to her
an infant   touched and held and rocked
        the soft scalp covering
the top of her head is guarded at all times   a skin
        to skin closeness
intimacy fading as our daughter grows farther from my body
        in okatoks alberta
an erratic rests in a field   rock born high in the rockies
        slid away from the body
of the mountain   held in glacial ice then dropped
        at the base of these foothills
our daughter   two months old   lying across my outstretched arms
        the feel of her skin
the flow of the land interrupted by a rock rolling over the face
        of what would become alberta
the mountain's memory of gravity heaving that huge sliver
        of quartzite and siltstone
to rest near highway 7   rock broken into three crouched bodies
        the wind is always a presence
and in okatoks where this erratic is not supposed to be
        fields are open
and diagonal seams of rock reach skyward   nothing is bigger
        on this undulating land
where rock breaks open the earth's expectations and the sun
        burns white   burns all blue
out of the heavens   a wind path in the field pulls us forward
        we are held inside our finite bodies
the land all around rolling open   the intimacy
        of sky and earth
and this ten thousand year old body
        of rock
a child is a sudden presence in the world
        the big rock   an irregularity
an intrusion in the soft bed of the field   we stand
        on its sinuous blanket   three flat bones
at the crown   her pliant skull not yet closed to the sky

bow river bending

nothing

I am the world to her
and nothing
I am what keeps her
alive   I am everything
or I am a thing
in front of what her brain does not
recognize as vision   light falling
on what is before her
eyes   the pattern
on the couch   my shoulder   the folds
of my hair   my ear   my eyes
my face is everything in the world and not
separate from my smell   not separate
from her smell smeared into me   the sounds
my breathing and heartbeat make   music
in the air of the room   trucks and cars
at the car wash and at all hours
people plug round gold
coloured dollars into a slot and soap
and wax and rinse their cars   humming
preoccupied by the suddenly beautiful surfaces
where brown road dust gathers itself into a thin sauce
of mud and cascades down windshields
under the force of water
washed
and in winter   the heat
of the spray splays into separate beads of ice
fog and billows white
across the black reach of the parking lot
and all of this is inside
my daughter who is pressed to my skin
drinking in my every vision as I sit out
the hours of night and I remain
nothing
a raft in her infant hunger   an appendage
of her body   an expression of her own
absolute will   the milk
at the edge of her dawning
consciousness reaches her mouth
bathing her tongue in a world
containing only herself

washed

my skin is dry and textured like sandpaper for love
of the sleeping baby   my husband's skin has become foreign
his body a forgotten country where I lived
and breathed eons
before this garden of a daughter   lungs
filled with the life blood of oxygen   she knows my skin
the smell of my skin and my voice close to her ear
she knows my hands
and the hands of my husband   she knows
this haven we have made with our bodies

this girl alive for one hundred and eighty days
how many hours   how many breaths   how much air
has she pulled up into her lungs from that invisible
second after the cutting   when I was washed
in the blood of birthing as the wet petals
of her new lungs unfurled
in the arid air and she pushed
out that first drawn breath as a cry

begin again

I mean my skin is dry because I love her
my skin is dry because it is calgary alberta
and I love her   the city is made
into something other than it was   the name
peter lougheed on the side of the hospital
becoming what anchors me to earth   this name
the place where my daughter took her first breath

the city's northeast quadrant
the labour and delivery floor
a window thrusting west to mountains
a single wild rose
her first gift

my skin is dry because it is calgary and it is january and my skin

my skin is dry because I will not touch anything
to my skin that is not pure
soap or water   anything that could mar
her porous body   her skin a permeable
sheath   a breathing veil absorbing
the world   dust sand grit soil soot
air penetrating her open mouth
throat   lungs and heart
internal organs so lately housed
within me when I was her outer armour
and my skin and muscles and bones
were barriers to the outside and she was
an internal body hoarding
her own half-children
in the curved clasp of her ovaries

and I want all skin contact to be pure

my milk   my body and blood
and the blood of this family

I remember the shelter of my arms
my husband breathing beside me
a thunderstorm wrapping itself around us
the week our daughter was born

that thirsty air bathed in memory
of the high gold lettering   *peter lougheed*
catching sun on the south side
of the hospital   washed in calgary
on this high altitude
body of land pressuring the sky
caught in the incessant
flypath of westerly winds

and the air   this dry air   the city
where our daughter first drew breath

writing mother

I only know language
has been leached of what I want
to say I only know what my body means
to her she is without language her body
embodies it the shape
she takes in my arms her language of unlocked
vowels soft blending of the softer
letters how they are held in her mouth
released on her exhaled
breath I know there is no language
for what I want to say no language
for mother and child that hasn't been
washed and rinsed and spun
to dry so many times that what is left
has paled and this bleached
version is all I have
to work with the words
left to me are not muscular
enough for what I want
to say pictures of young pink
mothers and their young
pink children is all
our language allows but I want
to write
I want to write
motherhood my own
state of motherhood
but the word has slipped
so far from the truth
of my daughter's body in mine
in the room where she sleeps in the centre
of the house the word *mother*
the word *daughter* the image
of us together worn
away to a light
translucent scrap of nothing
leaving me without
expression leaving me worn out

words   spent words
their gloss and value lost
through years   hundreds
of years of being fumbled
and fingered   rubbed and made
pretty and flimsy
my own language lightweight
and this pale pink decorative
candy floss mass of words unable
to support the weight of what I want
to say about the slant
of light on my daughter's
face   so I sink
into the soft sponge of hopeless
cliché   to write about women
holding babies   the river
bending and moving beneath
the ice outside is something
that cannot be said
something that will drown
in its banality   but the bodies
of children   the faces of mothers
are blurred into meaning and the river
and the circle of the week that brings us
together are all true
but without language

outside history

a room becomes beautiful with women
  women's hands and the heads
    of their babies   mouths latched to the mothers'

      bodies   the bow river

turns a corner   bends outside windows
  where women hold children   flawless
    infants utterly without

      history

their thin shaking cries twisting at us
  making our milk come in
    until the babies are quieted at the breasts of the

      mothers in the blank

muted comfort of two in the afternoon
  in this community   this solid
    circle before it is shaken apart

      with girlish hands cupped

to secretive ears   before our babies wean
  and we revert to the turncoat girls
    we might have been   whatever

      loyalties we might have held

showing their sieve-like flaws
  this room of women
    turns as sudden as leaves

      in fall   a translation

takes place and we are reduced
  to the language of girls
    language of women

      before men   girls in school

appraising   relishing each other's reflections
  in high school mirrors where careful
    lip gloss was layered on   when we leaned into

      our reflected selves

and what we said was encoded
  in closed adolescence
    it is this language that has come

      sharp and glittering

into the room and I don't know
  who has let this fretful
    girl into our circle but here

      she is   reminding us

of ourselves   our former lives
  making us see differently and start
    comparing   but not yet

      in this story   mothers

are identical women infused
  in a honeyed viscous oblivion
    identities eroded to a flawless blank

      bend in a river

where we merge into each other   into the desires
  of our hungering babies
    their desires becoming our only desire

      this blood

the blood that makes us women holds us down
  to the now   to this moment
    making us for this time and place

        only women   only bodies

gripping a small portion of this
world these children
these other

women we easily have become

in a room welded to a wall of windows
offering up a river
that flows through this day

we are kept

in suspension chinook sweeping down
mountains melting everything we were
all accumulation disappearing under

the clothesline narrative

warmth of this wind and we sit shaken out
of our girlhood selves girlhood
histories blowing past us as we dismiss

a future we can't imagine

today we see nothing beyond our bodies
or the bodies of our children
we have no need to rise any higher

than our own head and hands

we open our fingers and allow this room
and these sweet fickle
friendships to flow through us

and take root

translation

the window is feminine
because it is open
and transparent but the milk
the milk is masculine though it flows
from the feminine
however it is defined
why can't I walk
outside the poem   why can't
I talk alongside the poem
as it is projected onto this screen
of recollection   silent and slow motion
as I point   as I stop
this memory loop   the women that we were
the women met every week
and every week we learned
more about women
being mothers   I don't want to play
with language which is a masculine noun
though its utterance   its flow
over the tongue is
feminine in our country's other
mother language   though each word
we weave through our children's
first memory of language is forever
masculine   I only want
to point out the women
sitting beside the open feminine wall
of windows in the weekly café
where we watch each other
learn how to mother   I want to look
I want to step outside memory
I want to freeze us within
the poem's frame and really
see us but I can't recognize
what I was   what we all were
when we first closed

into a clutch of mothers
around these new lives
these new bodies
so recently inside
our emptied
masculine bellies

trading birth war stories

inductions taking agonizing days or babies coming too fast and two said they ripped badly despite episiotomy and one said after she'd delivered they took the epidural tube out and the doctor sewed her back together without anaesthetic for fifty minutes while she screamed and one said she was pushing and had such pain she thought she had delivered but the nurse said it was only a contraction and stuck her hand up during the next one *everyone who walked by had their fingers in me* she said *bring on the plumber and let him have a go as well* and another said her husband was eating a banana *take that fucking banana out of your mouth it's making me sick* she said she threw up the whole six hours she pushed her son out and one said she birthed her daughter with only her doctor and boyfriend who held and comforted and rubbed her hard all through the back labour and another said her nurse sat in the corner knitting and looking at the monitor saying *there's no way you are ready why are you even in bed?* and the baby coming all in an unexpected rush and one said she had such fear of the pain because it was the second time and she knew what to expect but she was also afraid of morphine demerol epidural and even a planned c section she was just so afraid but there was nothing to be done because the baby was in there and had to come somehow

riley park

cheerios   wheat crackers   figs
cut into four pieces   slices
of pale peeled cucumber wrapped
in saran so the crackers stay
dry   small squares
of yellow cheese   an inch
by an inch and round breton
crackers in flat orange
containers and square soda
biscuits and animal cookies
a banana and grapes halved
lengthways to prevent
choking   small plastic glasses
of orange juice cut
with three parts
water and topped
with purple spill
proof spouts   plastic bags
crushed into backpack
pockets for diapers
and wet cloths
in safeway bags
talk of how far along
someone is and talk
of who might be
and who will be
we take in the shapes
of each other's
bodies and count
the weeks and drink in
the sight of our children
running in larger
and larger circles around us
on the impossible
expanse of grass

morning

notice the fury of morning is not
what gets written   books to be packed   the loose
litter of marked papers   a clock slices
off scant minutes in the search for the lost
travel coffee mug   an apple for school
break   the baby running   the slap of her
bare feet on the cold floor   baby running
and falling   my husband and I howling
all about who should have been where and when
now just ten more minutes until the race
against the car radio   I'm punching
station after station for a song to
lurch me forward seven or eight minutes
on memorial drive to the centre
street bridge with five or six inches between
car and car   car and bridge railing   all this
fury subsiding by riverfront drive
the long slow curve past chinatown   down first
street under the train bridge and the turn on
eighteenth avenue and I'm here but it's
day to day and it's mundane and it's not
poetry or how poetry gets made

breathing paper

what will be left of me when I am dead
paper   the flimsy delicacy of paper
diaries and letters and the slim
published body
of work   paper that is subject
to water or fire or gradual erosion
from time itself   thinning
year after year until the paper
I am printed on goes back
to pulp and wood   back
to the very air breathing in wider
and wider circles around the limbs
and leaves of trees reduced
for paper   the objects
we own   have owned in our lives
are not stable   our beds
and bookshelves passed on   what hands
will touch our discarded curtains
wear clothes cast off our bodies
eat from our dishes   in time
our objects will scatter and hold
nothing more of us   what will be
left of me when I am no longer
breathing   no longer of this place
my tracings on paper and the living
breathing body of my daughter
who lies on the floor
above me   my daughter
will walk the level
earth I am
buried beneath   she will hold
her inherited objects
and after her   a daughter   living
child of her body and another
daughter and another
forward into memories not yet
lived through   just as I hold
my mother's body in mine
something of her and she holds
her mother and her mother

holds the flesh and bone
and blood of the woman
who braved the ocean
at the beginning of another
century and all of us have touched
have passed through each other
on the way to the future

pure blood

I am cooking for my daughter
red blood smell of meat rolling between my palms

the richness of this flesh   I love
the blood on my hands

yet years ago I gave up meat for lent
how it was to be without

meat and how it was to eat meat again after forty days
I remember I ate lamb stew and steak and roast

beef   I ate ground spiced pork until I couldn't
bear the thick fat taste any longer

fifteen years later I'm forming meatballs
I want fresh food for her   I want

only meat
pure meat

nothing else mixed in
how I am inside her

and she is inside me   how we are
conjoined   my husband

swings her into the air on her screamed laugh
the mother inside

each daughter   my mother inside me
that signature of flesh

my mother's mother so imbedded she has a perfect
bodily memory of her own mother's near drowning

swung like a carcass into the lachine canal   *swimming lessons*
bellowed her father   locking the priest out

when he was slow to pay a debt
barred from his own parish-paid wooden church

whole family locked out   locked away from god
two generations later my mother recovering

religion in a cookbook
I remember the one year we shared

the forty days abstaining
from blood   abstaining from meat

then the bright easter morning
breaking the fast together

roof of clouds net of stars

barren

my nausea over fried eggs is wishful
thinking my circling of possibility
of possibly fertile days
symptomatic of want
of wishing for time
to stop dripping away

my polish student explaining absence
I have pregnant lucky young
woman *you will have a canadian*
baby I say
for the rest of the day rest of the week
I keep her in my sight seven weeks gone
hidden under her sweater and shirt and layers
of skin flesh fat
and bone is the beginning of what I want
another beginning

late december is an uphill struggle
twelve months heavy engorged
memory circling in as starvation
each day with its border of darkness
thickening at evening and morning
coming later
and later thin dry
snowflakes open the grey
white sky and sting
our uplifted faces
while we want nothing
but to cover ourselves
with gluttony
and sleep and the absolute
darkness at solstice sugar
beaten into softened butter
beginning each recipe as we reach
the barren end of the calendar
when we are left wishing
oven-warm baking could sustain us
through the cold through the dark

then the shock of christmas
lights in the sharp dead
of night   stars standing out
sweet

we need to have our deaths written

we need someone to write out death because death
is leaking into every cup we raise to our mouths
and death grows in sharp green spikes of pure will
from each fissure in the dry earth weeks before we take time
to turn soil for gardens we have planned   death crouches
inside our own uncertain skins   gasping back hungry breath
for the trigger that will spiral us into its everlasting arms
death is grinning and corkscrewing in the wind breathing
through us our whole lives   death sits
sipping bitter coffee in a cadillac parked
across the street   spinning numbers on the car radio
music illuminated under those exacting fingers
until our song fills the absence of that space
only for a moment   we need someone to tell us

how death was at the wedding   how death was deep cancer
inside my cousin   gluttonous in her bones   her hip bone
glowed with it as she dragged on her cigarette until the tip
was a single red eye of longing   at her sister's wedding
her lungs reached out and swooning   took death inside
the cancer a kind of blue sword
fish jumping from bone to bone to lung to throat
to her last words   her last breath
six o'clock on a sunday morning   we need to have this
death down on paper   we need to have our lives remembered
touched first with a fingertip then cupped   trembling
for half a breath in the palm of a hand then written
with ink that won't run even when the white
of the wedding registry is wet with rain

we need death examined as body after body is washed
and laid into the ground   we need to remember children
crying babies in their mothers' arms were told to stay
at that wedding   their cries a kind of joy
we couldn't unravel   we need to know rice
is thrown for children   a handful of rice
equalling life as it continues welling up in women
despite years of spinning clocks and car crashes and cancer
and heart attacks and massive strokes at ridiculously early ages

life fires back lingering yellow heat inside the blood
of our mothers   we need someone to know this   we need
someone to look without fear into the faces of the newly born
only now emerging from that soft covering of darkness
and write what all this life means

scatter

darkness has grown bolder   a whole day lost
to baking   my hands full of flour pushing
the ball of dough again into the cold
marble bread board   early january
and the ragged ribbon of afternoon
darkness has blurred   has softened   a snowstorm
blowing up hard from the southwest   the news

from the world outside is given to us
in the green glow of the weather channel
watched like religion by men in my house
their need to know the conditions over
the whole country as they stalk from window
to window   work all four sides of the house
their need to push the inevitable

into the mind's half-forgotten back room
as they get ready   mixing gas and oil
for the snow blower   this whole cold country
coiled under the same steely sky   I punch
my fist through the heart of the tripled dough
scatter a furious storm of flour
for another bout of heavy kneading

I watch the indistinct sky   afternoon
succumbs to veiled night   a reliquary
of last light   winter sky fluctuating
and I coax bread to life   light ascending
from this immaculate body   the fierce
wish for spring stalks each frost-gripped room   this day
lost to baking   this day my hands are full

february

I'm so lonely for him I can't think of it I'm sick
of myself sick of the rabid machinery of my mind
slipping into the same rut of worry over the rudderless
calendar of my body when the starburst lily an early
easter gift opens sticky and pink trumpeting
its scent at me aggressive across the kitchen I want
my husband home with me not halfway
up the map barred by road closures on the radio
reports of how much snow fell in such
and such a place on the highway
I've memorized I want him
home I want that single perfect instant
when my egg releases invisible and I open
to him and I no longer have to want
but hunker down
and wait

jack box

I'm talking conception
the secret end of winter with every star
burning above our bed   I'm talking climbing pleasure
finger and toe holds on the jerking
ladder to heaven as we force life   rising
bread scorching the oven   smoke filling the house
snow blurring all windows on this first day of march
gestational age twelve hours
inside my unknowable darkness where I have to believe
there is a secret free-falling in a uterine star field
a due date already branding my calendar

blood upon implantation
in the story   germination occurs in darkness
overnight seeds tossed from the bedroom
taking root in flower boxes   the magic
complete upon waking   his seed anchors
this bed   swelling to a stalk and folding into twins
placenta and embryo
tendrils coil the hook of heaven   becoming a pulse
of cells enticed to the rich red bed of the uterus
I am becoming an envelope of skin
wrapping around a starting point
an invisible password weaving into my body
my body a giant   a dream-dwelling
with its sudden roof of clouds

jacked
I've tried to take all the jack story and his magic stalk
piercing clouds where a giant is craving the scent
is holding eggs heavy as gold
I've tried to take the forgotten cow traded
on the road and the handful of seeds thrown
by the mother   you remember she tossed
magic away and I am wondering
if it was seed or soil
performing the miraculous sowing
the mystery of the five-pointed star
seedbed of a bisected apple held in my hand

fee-fie-foe-fum is the smell of our mingled blood
is the flowering vine slithering upward
castle in the sky
life catching fire

skyhook
clouds and roofs and beds centring the story
I am trying to plant
what is taken on trust becomes magic
a cow traded for seed has no place in this writing
except to honour the milky way   a life giver
I want to sew a net of stars
milking an ocean of constellations
I want to be bathed in light   in milk
but in jack's story   there is no need for mother
and her loss of the milk cow   a hungry
searching rootlet is how the beginning of a child
climbs into the sky   am I the giant
or is the roof of my uterus the dreamland
where eggs are gold
and plotted through the sliding trajectory
of the body's calendar   his seeds and my riches
my eggs reaching something I can't figure
mythology breaking down while he's jacked halfway
up heaven's ladder   lying in wait for that gold
that goose who can't stop laying

his jack   my box
this primitive urge below the skin of consciousness
we say primitive because we cannot explain
our need of each other's bodies and my need
my growing need to be pregnant
flesh is willed
we go on that   live by it
we cannot know if we have lit life in our darkness
and proof of what we have done will not come
until my flesh is forced
to expand   my skin made to stretch

baking day

apple-spiced bread smouldering in the oven
kitchen windows open to pull smoke out
the loaf rises too high and it keeps growing   it's snowing
and snowing   outside a white blur
inside my kitchen   it's warm from the baking
I pull that loaf from the heat and remember the love
we made last night   when he touched me
my body was a bright burr of feeling
a five-pointed star
there are no true words   all words   all knowledge
smudged out of my head   out of my mouth
how we were nothing
but twined flesh ascending   how our pleasure
penetrated the very peak
of the roof   how we were released
into the upper air and how
we made our son that night

blue ribbon

comet hale-bopp arching through a small square
of sky above the bluff on the black drive
home and hours before the nurse in her light
blue uniform pushed open the door without
knocking   her face a constellation
of freckles   her black hair clasped
in a child's moon-shaped clip and she clutched
my test with its thin blue ribbon baby
barely begun   the arching firmament
of my body where a child is not yet
a naked eye object   comet hale-bopp
last seen by slaves raising pyramids
won't shoot past again for two thousand years
this is the vernal equinox   my love

a child in our arms by christmas morning

inscription

my identity is made of paper
I am laced together with words
felted to fine thin sheets
compacted into what can be read
enmeshed fibres taking on shape   the body
fit into the substance of pregnancy   a skin

of words hosting this willed act pressed into the scant
wet flesh of meaning   the shore where the heat
the poem fires the white-sand
sheet of the body to be read
as a pregnant woman is written   where papyrus
puts down roots under a scripted wave of syntax

opening blank space   filling
incrementally with life   the female body
in a sea of open-mouthed vowels and shards
of consonants   the sky
a torn open manuscript
a cloudburst of nouns

and verbs raining down as hard
handwriting hammering out a second skin
the sustained black workings of type
incised onto the unconscious blank page
with glossaries ebbing up to the skin
surface and out to the top margins   I want paper

embedded with language   plankton-like letters
boldly ripening into meaning   words swollen
floating all around me and there is my need to write
out to the edges   my skin
bearing the inscription of nascent words as paper
is flecked with markings forming text and read

as a wrapping of self parcelled out to paper over
these wet walls of pregnancy   floating my body
above and outside ordinary space
teasing out a second heart with its blood
anchor already inside me and I revel in this shift
from singular body to maternal wrapping   my finest paper

in the end

in the beginning I am myself
in the end I am tethered to my son's placenta
in the end I am only a uterus
amplified to the size of a child I am only body
head and heart my belly and brain cleaved
two hemispheres
one of the world one floating above
the baseness of body
my body is everything for the son
about to be forced from me into the cold
noise of oxygen at the second of his birth

a 38-week-old body that is all I am

I behold my breadth
of a belly spanning the long
slim space of a full-length
mirror I am
surprised at how little
is left of me in the gravity
of these last flourishing weeks my self
my former self split off
set adrift
and I will be surprised at my future
son's terror over this photograph
when told he is inside
how he will run to the mirror to find his
face and body are his own
not trapped
under my stretched skin

but it's me I'm the one ensnared
I am absorbed into the snarled
bloodlines of my son I am the bait
his need has hooked what I eat
and breathe is absorbed
into his very centre crossing the placenta
that oval flesh boat
that has been his inborn twin bonded
to his orbit by an equator

of blood since his beginning   in the end
nights are infused with insomnia
and the ends of movies on tv   blue veins
pulsing under the white volcanic surface
of my skin   breasts small
beside this eruption of belly
everything small
beside what my body has become

I am only body   only doctor's
tape circling   measuring seven days' growth
and I measure every step   how many to take
how many till rest   in the end I crave cold
autumn air   my daughter and I counting
our steps in the back alley   remembering
my mother-in-law desperate to slip a hat
onto our girl's head when she was small
and we turned a corner into frozen foods
she'll catch a chill   as if chills gestated
deadly and invisible
over ice cream and orange juice

now leaves are drenched in yellow
and stitched to the clean
expanse of blue overhead
sharp with the whistling
visible breath of late october
I put my head down and push

in the end   there will be labour and delivery
and an infant needing the unbroken clock
of constant wakefulness   I push into wind
whispering through vivid trees
in my head   my voice
counts down the days

sweet rock

my son is a press of bones under my ribs
a rounded rock of sugar seeping into my blood
I am bones grating flesh and fat beneath skin
straining round me like an elastic coat   I am a tightening
knot of knees and elbows and a jagged hunch
of shoulder blades as I steep into full term
immobility   barely loosening in the steam of 3 am baths
I bathe in darkness to ease migraines and the thin
hot wire of insomnia night
after night   then jerking awake
to the alarm sounding 1 30 for that small
meal to keep ketones down and blood balanced
but fasting sugars are high and stay high
I pinch my drum-tight skin six times
a day and insert silver insulin needles and test
and test my sugars   sweet round
numbers falling away on the glucose meter
then remembered in slim blue
books and fed into my hospital file   fat
and growing fatter as weeks melt down
and my inner walls weaken
under the heavy undertow of pre-labour
my son's head is ripening rock candy
rooting me to the jagged night-time creak
of hardwood floors as I use a wall
for a crutch and wander the thin
darkness of these expectant rooms
huddled tight inside november

vaulted

before the sun swims up the ladder
of the world   before day spills over
to flood this northern city   our son floats
and fights against the overlay of skin
and flesh I took on for the voyage
this hull   this clenched tight ark
keeping him close

my husband's hands mark the arch
of my body in the last grey moments
before daybreak

I feel our son when I touch you

water breaking me open

leaking amniotic fluid
two weeks early cramping lower
back pain starting at 2
or 3 continuous leaking and thin
streaks of blood 3
49 a twenty second
contraction 3 53
twenty more seconds
3 59 thirty
to forty seconds 4 oh
5 ten seconds does that one
even count 4 oh 9 for a good
twenty five seconds am I in labour
4 14 didn't time
seemed longer 4 18
another twenty second
contraction I should wake
him we should pack
a bag 4
21 forty five the longest yet
we should call his parents
to come for our girl
I should prepare 4 25
I should prepare twenty
or twenty five seconds but mild
I should prepare break
fast for her 4
32 forty seconds
4 38
twenty seconds we should
we should phone
the hospital 4 39
twenty seconds I think
we should phone I think
I don't think
I'm ready

6 23

hours before our son begins
to pull air into his mouth and his lungs
are still and folded closed like flesh
coloured bat wings hanging in the jointed
cage of his ribs   I am jolted
by a contraction I can't forget   6 23
square blue-green numbers glowing
on the car's dashboard are etched
into my pain   negating
the way your mind is supposed to fill
only with the air of your labour
breathing   as if gut-level
breathing will annul the ordeal
6 23 has me
pitching forward into the snap
and pull of the shoulder belt
and my sweating palms slip
gripping the flat brown slab
of the dash as I suck shallow lung
fulls of this cold november morning
air which will transmute into blood
the last hours of blood bonding me
to our unborn son

first time

the whole thing is too much has gotten ahead way ahead of me
I want the epidural I want to get out of this I don't know how
long it will take in real time *hydrated* the nurse says *you need to be*
totally hydrated and hangs a full fat IV bag from the pole I am
bound to *when this bag is empty we will call an anaesthetist*
a horrible moment between contractions I look up
and look up again at that huge clear bag hanging above
my pain pulsing through me one slow drip after drip *don't*
look at it don't look at the bag she drifts away how can
I not look I can't stop can't stop looking I look
after every slamming into my gut contraction I am
standing beside the pole I can't stand to have
his hands on me I shove his hands away from my body
then grab him back and try to push pain out
through my mouth pain everywhere pain staining the four close
walls of the room pain hot pain fanning out into the molecules
of air I gasp back down my throat scorching
my lungs my belly my goddamn guts and throbbing
throbbing through my stubborn uterus and searing down
both legs the knees a red centre of pain planted pain finally
burning out through the soles of my bare feet wet
with sweat I force pain out on my screamed breath and it rolls
back in again and I am not separate from it I am the pain
and it is me it is all I am I breathe pain drag it in I am not
separate not separate as invisible silent nurses flicker through
the room I am not separate from the walls or the cold
floor I am not separate from the dripping the endless
dripping IV bag not separate from the soft beige of the plaid
shirt he is wearing as I grip his arms and scream I scream
so much I feel faces peering in through the flimsy curtain
of a door and after each bout I crumple I completely crumple
into his arms sobbing like our daughter in the throes of some
childhood despair and I hold her carefully in my mind
I hold that jagged picture of our girl as I cry the way
she cries keening and shaking and somehow she is here
right here in the hot centre of this storm of birthing
we made her brother and we made her and now
her father and I are clutching each other as we are blasted
by each black red contraction we are all in the same

boat the whole family the four of us even our son
hours from his first breath we hold on and we cry
we breathe and we wait for the air of the birthing
room to cool and enter his small wet
lungs for the first time   first time ever

post op

I had to navigate aisles of shivering
red-coloured babies born too soon and buzzing
emergency approximations of lungs and heart
holding them in sterile bubbles of the living
I had to negotiate the nurse at intensive care
hand scrubbing waved away in an indulgent
gesture of welcome   how she took me
by the arm as though strolling   past pulsing
code red lights   heat lamps   huddled rocking mothers

I had to be taken by wheelchair while still leaking
blood   still wearing the half gown of the recently
operated   when his body was taken from mine
and doctors   nurses   my husband and his parents
all held my son   I had to lie open
and unconscious and hours after he entered
the cold of this world   I pressed and pressed
the brown button beside the bed I could not roll over in

the first time I saw him was in a polaroid

until I am pushed past all
that is urgent and I am greedy
for him   reach for him finally
finally hold my boy

and I am delivered

drinking the light

blood mother

in art   god sucks life
from the breast of the virgin
a hard breast held like a lean pear
in his hands   this picture is christened
madonna of humility
as if in giving life   she is drained
of power   yet god
grows fat on the milk that is
mirrored in the painted
air above her as stars
of the milky way decorate ceilings
in church   her name is humility
as if the milk is not everything
this wash of milk from the human mother
as if it is not gifted from the body
of a woman grafted to the god of the word
as if this is not miracle enough
these red and gold images stain
the wood of the icon   etching the holy
made flesh   the christ   the child
is grateful at the breast
of the queen of heaven   god
is overwhelmed with the sweet
goodness of she
who takes away the hurt
of his hunger   his huge
eternal blood mother shrugging
away the painted halo
as she draws her child
to herself and allows him
to put away
the pain of the world

december   edmonton

light is everything
for mere fleeting minutes
my three-week-old son drinks
in the light   hands
embracing and circling
air flowing invisible
as ice above his head
the window a vessel
of light but there is still
the dormant north-
facing kitchen with its cold frame
stack of breakfast dishes   curled
peelings of potatoes   carrots
and turnips   compost
for the inert grey-white of my raw
december garden to be transfigured
into a solid vegetable body of ice
before the white tides of winter swell
what can still be seen of the sky
before the only presence of light
in the world is the fluttering
illumination of falling
snow under street lights
there is still darkness
and this kitchen   there is
the whole of a punishing
winter to be pushed through
before the stilled earth
stirs again and the arctic heart
of my garden softens as light begins
to come back to us   the very idea of north
pulsing here in the throat and burning
cold under the palm of my hand
pressed to the morning's white
gilding of frost on this western window
that each afternoon becomes
a container for the day's last brilliance
bathing my son   light transient
as a blessing   as the softest touch
on the skin of his face and hands

a moment before the world
rolls over to ready itself for the still
of night closing like a fist frozen
over this   the most northerly place
we've ever lived

accumulation

the sudden additive nature of all things
how the puckered assemblage of soiled laundry
surges   reaching the tip
the top of the wicker basket
growing up the bolster of bedroom wall
blankets   sheets   woollen socks
shirts   pants   tops   bottoms
stain and spill   spew and sweat telling our story

we are at the end of a day that won't end
and our only thoughts are of stealing sleep
in this clamped closed post-partum nest
so much without thought   the bedroom forced
out of time with its dark felt contours
and a clock that lies to us

where sleeping is the same as waking
waking the same as walking
the wailing baby and night
weeps again into day
and the tent of clothing slouches
up the wall where our crushed
softened   day-old clothes hold us
hold a memory of us in their indistinct folds

and what is clean
what is pristine is dropped at our doorstep
diapers   one day out of seven
before first light   vague
contours of the laundered sack   soft
sculptured sentinel left like a gift

another week stacked and folded
in this close den of a closet
where my own needs
are less   shapeless
shirts   jeans suddenly
roomy now that my son's need
is nursing my shrinking

body into less
than the pride
I carried out in front
for what seemed so long
and is deflated
now that he is here

this boy we are learning
to love

we hoard the loosely knit-
and-purl minutes   we accumulate
unbraided hours and days
blunt and toothless as wet wool

we watch air diffuse
into swirling strands of unending
immediacy and days undulate
taking on slow weight as weeks
unravel into months

things of the world

the same motion a dozen times a day
lifting my shirt and latching my son's mouth
to the breast that will give him everything   I am
staring at trees   trees mean everything

lifting my shirt and latching my son's mouth
trees I see from my living room   I stare
at those swaying limbs which mean the world
I'm as rooted as those trees   only care

to watch swaying   my head fills with nothing
my thoughts close up   nothing but blank
balloons   a white-out blankets my mind
the same motion a dozen times a day

my mind empties and I give him
everything   my thoughts float   transparent
circles of air   a dozen times a day   thoughts
stopped at the ceiling   thoughts I mean

rising blank balloons I mean to write down
never do   all action is of the body
and thought is cleaved from flesh
everything I was drained into the marrow

of my own milk   I'm marooned
all is body   nothing more
than this narrow dart of milk
I'm unable to hold more than one

thought inside this mind   this body
cloistered   tethered tight to the house
by the lock of his mouth   the same
motion a dozen times a day

desperate

my son's stomach and mouth and cry uproots
uproots me from my black sludge of sleep
my daughter picks scabs from every question
unanswerable questions a hundred
hundred times until I want to scream
curse in hard-boiled frustration she can't
understand   how I won't manage to string
I can't string together two or three words
this twisted knot of morning   how I hang
on each radio broadcast for smoothness
adult sounds   my daughter wanting me
to read the same story for the third
fifth   eighth time this morning   I'm captive
on the couch as she picks up book after
book   slamming each as close to her brother's
close to her brother's head as she dares
snack time to be tackled and all errant
juice boxes to be fished from under the
rumpled swamp of a bed   diapers
again crayon marks to be scrubbed
from walls tattooed with dirty
fingerprints smeared into a
into a rorschach revealing something
I don't know what   lunch   thank god nap
naptime then my rush   my desperate stop
watch race towards something   some future
second frozen on the stove-top clock
I need something   need to get
some little thing done   a broom
rasping across the rice
and kraft dinner encrusted floor
a letter or half
a paragraph of a book I no longer
no longer have the brains for
all narrative thread lost
that ability to navigate text
lost   all connective tissue
so lacerated   lines splinter
apart   a jumble of letters
I can't restring

silence

my silence is the silence
of mothering   the blank pages
are peeled and sliced
apples   cheese and crackers
then chicken broth   bread
and butter   sweeping that doesn't
lessen the dirt and sand
brought in on boots   time
dropped through thin-throated
glass as moments throng
into days given over
to children
my hands are in dishwater
and poetics   the habit
of metaphor folded away
into laundry   diapers
the picking and picking
up of a hundred small
plastic toys   nothing
is committed
to paper   my words flash
blast into
the air and broadcast invisible
patterns   sink silent
and disappear

I hate these poems

their lattice of wording   a void
not saying what I want   not capturing
how I love the kids and how they chain me
to themselves   these poems cannot
convey the corroding anger of my house arrest
or my amazement and gratitude at the trick
ridiculous and contradicting
trick of mothering   I think if I could write
and rewrite   I could draw everything
back into focus

but there are holes in this web and meaning
is not making it to the page
I hate these pages   they are nothing
they are not equal to this mothering
life which cannot be written   each sharp
snapshot is over exposed in sentiment

mothers are edgeless
soft yielding flesh   mothers are sand
toys and bottles of sun
screen and extra hats against sunburn
mothers are cheap strollers
stuck in slush ruts at the isolated centres
of winter intersections   mothers are not in the world
not the real world existing somewhere above
this mess and noise of children

I cannot make any of it
fit onto paper   there is the revelation
of a child bathed in mid-morning
shadow and there is the want
the need for an infant we fear
will stop breathing deep in the night and the aching
exhaustion of endless colicky crying and our desperate
desperate craving to covet and protect

there is the radiant love
we bear them

yet there are no words   nothing
right once written down   our frantic
devotion to them has to go unsaid as does the furious
buzz saw in our heads when they won't be still
stop fighting or begging one more cookie

the outside world is abstract
off limits and it is only
the food the cleaning the dressing the washing the rocking
the caring for
that is real

each task is multiplied
by a thousand   time thrusting
onward and rolling backward
a stuttering series of screeching jerks
forever in the wrong gear
yet righting itself   miraculously
righting itself each morning

born again

suddenly my son is separated from the landscape of my body
suddenly weaned   I am no longer part of that single being
mother and child   I am no longer sustaining
no longer food

a white-grey curtain closing between us one morning and he is
drinking not sucking   drinking first mouthfuls of juice
and not milk   never again the milk of my body as I hold him
and we dissolve

into the slow shift of morning as two separate bodies
mine is given back to me as my son is born
reborn away from me by the thick
veined months compressing to years

my body is mine again
but I am unthroned from where I reigned
until this day   beneficent   adjunct to my son
immobile

like a wooden icon   our lady of the living room couch
and I am shifting around for the shelter
of a new meaning   wanting to fathom
how a finite run of milk-coloured days

marked our truncated history   in time
each child weans me from the mouth and there is no ritual
and it is faced as another birthing   another umbilical cutting
as my daughter cut herself off from me

how she slipped the thinnest wedge of empty space between us
rolled away like the rock rolling away
from the closed cave on the day
of the resurrection

my daughter pushed me away so she could face outward
face the room and the world beyond the room
that held   until weaning
our single body

puzzle

our bodies are riddled
with meaning until we are nothing
but body   meaning slapped over
our skins   layered on like an extra coat
of paint   all our years colouring
shaping us   dragging us down
to earth   the puzzle of women
beyond age and beauty
undefinable
what the female body is   has been
and is becoming is the question
is the answer we are held to
our context in the world
defined by the body that contains us
as if we are held completely
inside our very coating
of the feminine   inside these
female bodies always
in flux   I mean a girl
or a woman or a pregnant
woman or an ageing
or old woman becoming
a definable point
on the body's drifting map

gravel

when the gravel of rage is tearing
out my throat the clock is ticking a boot
won't go on a kid's foot hat or mitt
or scarf is lost or hair hasn't been combed
or is snarling with tangles or breakfast
is wrong or the socks don't feel
right or I haven't yet gulped enough
coffee for the caffeine to have lifted me
out of my abrupt shift from 6 am
waking I'm raging at my kids and I hear
myself answering my mother *why did I*
have kids I shriek so they can hear me
and I hear my mother's voice and my voice
come together and see the hurt on my
children's white staring faces
my mother's cursing a snow bank
her 1968 blue beaumont stuck
some january past ramming
and ramming the gas pedal to rock
the car out of the ice she was
forming under spinning
wheels we kids in the back seat
not knowing our mother
was panicking at how much
needed to get done and her
car and the weather and these
children who had ended her
youth now giggling behind her
somehow the root of everything

biology

it's what we fought against all those years
this giving over to biology   to motherhood
in high school   girls who got pregnant were seen
as lost   as having lost themselves as they changed
as they swelled up   were swallowed up in biology
in high school we knew what to be
afraid of   we knew we could be lost
and we knew we had to hold that loss
back   had to push that urge   that biology
away from our bodies with our own
two hands   we had to hold those boys
back with all our strength

so all these years fighting *biology is destiny*
making the word *husband* suddenly rich
subversion and longing for the domestic
and sheltered seeming weak and womanly and taboo
middle class white heterosexist privilege
lingers on my lips and is written
in invisible letters hanging in shredded strips
of paper flapping like forgotten prayer
flags in the air above my bookshelf of nagging
unread books   my mother's 1970's voice
I am not a housewife
but here I am   succumbing
inside the walls of my house with the earth beneath it
and the air above it   all mine   I'm not sure
what I have become   what I have betrayed
in wanting this house and this husband to make me
a wife and these children to make me a mother

Eco-Audit

Printing this book using Rolland Enviro 100 Print instead of virgin fibres paper saved the following resources:

Trees	Solid Waste	Water	Air Emissions	Natural Gas
2	60 kg	5,678 L	132 kg	$9\,m^3$